BIRDS
HEADS & EYES

BIRDS
HEADS & EYES

Jack B. Kochan

STACKPOLE
BOOKS

Published by
STACKPOLE BOOKS
5067 Ritter Road
Mechanicsburg, PA 17055

Printed in the United States of America

10 9 8 7 6 5 4 3 2 1

First edition

Cover design by Caroline Miller and Tina Marie Hill

Library of Congress Cataloging-in-Publication Data

Kochan, Jack B.
    Birds—heads & eyes / Jack B. Kochan. — 1st ed.
        p.   cm.—(Birds)
    Includes bibliographical references.
    ISBN 0-8117-3005-0
    1. Wood-carving.   2. Birds in art.   3. Birds—Anatomy.   I. Title.
    II. Title: Birds—heads & eyes.
TT199.7.K633   1994
731'.832—dc20   94-29096
                                                                                                                        CIP

To my wife, for her loving patience throughout this endeavor

Contents

Foreword

My vocation is to care for orphaned and injured animals. More than two thousand birds and mammals are brought annually to the doors of the wildlife center where I work, treated, and, when feasible, returned to their natural habitats. Before I became a state and federally licensed rehabilitator, I spent years in research and study at a number of rehab centers to learn as much as possible about the creatures I would someday try to help. The time I spent reading, listening to lectures, and studying in the field gave me the background I needed for what has now been a twelve-year career.

One of the things that I keep learning is that I have much to learn. Just when I think I have seen it all, heard it all, read it all, *bam!*... I find something new. My library is filled with numerous periodicals, newsletters, files, slides, medical books, and photo journals, and I continually add to it.

I am eager to have Jack Kochan's new book, *Birds: Heads & Eyes*, on my shelf. Jack's book calls attention to the details our human eyes often miss. His fine illustrations capture the spirit of the birds and give insight into those areas which are most challenging to depict.

I know you will find Jack's book an invaluable help and inspiration as you work to create your artistic wild creatures.

Karen R. Groff

Preface

"What is it about the carving that attracts you most?" Ask this question of anyone who has attended a wildfowl carving show or competition, and you will almost invariably get the same answer: the head.

Most carvers and artists agree that the one part of a bird carving to draw first attention from an observer (or prospective buyer) is the head. The attitude, the symmetry, the lifelikeness, the expression, the character, are all first noticed in the head of a carving or painting. In fact the entire "essence of the species" is often totally captured in the head alone.

We humans recognize one another by the physical aspects of the head, especially the face, and perhaps have an ingrained response to look at the head of a bird for first recognition. Whatever the reason, it is the head of the bird that leaves a first and lasting impression on the observer. Therefore, much attention should be paid to exactness and detail when carving or drawing the head of a bird.

The head can depict the fierce glare that a hawk or an eagle displays, or the quiet aloofness often portrayed by many owls. It is the head of a bird that shows sleepiness, alertness, wariness, ferocity, or complacency.

With these thoughts in mind, I feel that the head is the most important part of bird anatomy that should be studied by the carver or artist. With a good understanding of head structure, the carver can better portray the essence of the species.

The primary purpose of this book is to give the carver or artist a broader knowledge and better understanding of bird anatomy. The more you know about any subject, the better you can portray it.

Although this book was written specifically with the carver in mind, it contains sufficient information so that it could be used as a primer for the budding ornithologist as well.

The topography of a bird's head is a surface map showing the various regions and boundaries.

ONE

Topography

In order to understand the anatomy of a bird's head, you must first become familiar with the topography, or the surface "map" of the head areas. The illustration below shows the various parts of a bird's head and identifies these parts by names that all ornithologists, carvers, and artists refer to when discussing a bird. There are as many sizes and shapes of heads as there are kinds of birds, yet all are similar in topographical orientation.

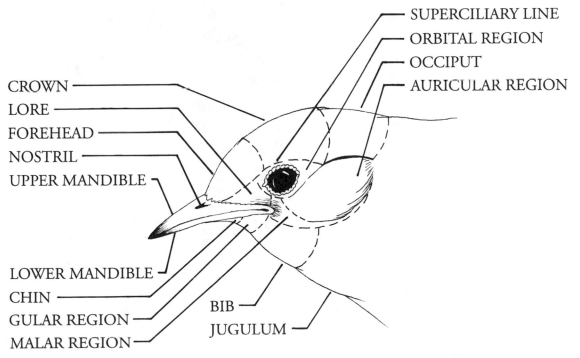

CROWN
LORE
FOREHEAD
NOSTRIL
UPPER MANDIBLE

SUPERCILIARY LINE
ORBITAL REGION
OCCIPUT
AURICULAR REGION

LOWER MANDIBLE
CHIN
GULAR REGION
MALAR REGION

BIB
JUGULUM

The forehead extends from the base of the upper bill to an imaginary line connecting the front corners of the eyes. The remaining upper part of the head is the crown, and the sloping back of the head is referred to as the occiput or hindhead. On a few species the crown has rather long feathers that tend to be more erect, thus creating a crest, as seen in the cardinal. Below the occiput to the bottom of the neck is the nape.

The cardinal has a crest of longer, more erect feathers on the crown.

The superciliary line is the lateral boundary of the forehead and crown. Between the base of the upper bill and the eyelids, just below the superciliary line, is the lore. On many species the lore contains whiskerlike feathers, which are quite prominent on most owls, while on other birds, such as herons, the lore is void of feathers.

Bristles growing from the lids of a rhea's eye give the bird the appearance of having eyelashes.

The side of the head is divided into three main regions: orbital, auricular, and malar. The orbital region includes the eye, the upper and lower eyelids, and the eye-ring. The eye-ring is a group of tiny feathers surrounding the eyelids. On certain species, the eye-ring is a distinctively different color than the surrounding areas. Birds do not have eyelashes but a few species have long hairlike feathers (bristles) growing on the eyelid that serve the same purpose. The ostrich is a good example of a bird with "eyelashes."

The auricular region surrounds the ear opening, which is concealed by a group of feathers known as the auriculars but are more commonly called the ear coverts.

The malar region, or "cheek," extends from the base of the lower bill, just below the lore, to a point just below and behind the ear. The feathers covering the malar region are often distinctively different in color than the surrounding feathers, thus creating a malar patch, more commonly called the mustache, as seen in the yellow shafted flicker.

The posterior (rear) corner of the eye, where the eyelids meet, is the temporal canthus, while the anterior (front) corner of the eye is the nasal canthus. Between the lower eyelid and the auricular region is the temporal region. This is a very small area and is usually considered part of the auriculars.

In the forked area on the underside of the lower bill is a feathered region called the chin. Directly below the chin is the gular region, which extends to an imaginary line connecting the angle of the jaws. Below the chin on the front of the neck is the bib. The bib is often a different color than the surrounding area, as in the ruby-throated hummingbird, and extends to the breast. These iridescent feathers on the bib of a hummingbird are known as the gorget and often extend far down and around the sides of the neck.

The brightly colored gorget of a hummingbird extends far to the sides of the head and neck.

In owls, there is the additional feature of the facial disc. The facial disc is a circlet of feathers surrounding the eye; it is more of a feather group than a structural feature but should be noted as a topographical difference.

The circlet of feathers in the orbital region of many owls creates a facial disc.

The bill itself has two main parts: the upper mandible, or maxilla, and the lower mandible. The centerline ridge of the upper mandible is called the culmen. The nostrils are located in the upper mandible, and on some birds there is a fatty, swollen structure that arches over the nostrils. This swollen structure is the operculum, or cere, and is prominent in pigeons. There is a fine line difference between an operculum and a cere although the two terms are usually thought to mean the same. A cere is normally harder in composition than the oper-culum and does not completely cover the nostrils, as seen in most hawks and falcons.

The line formed where the upper and lower mandibles meet is called the commissure, or gape, although the term gape is usually meant to mean the line along the edges of the open mouth.

The neck can be divided into four distinct regions. The aforementioned nape is the dorsal or top part of the neck, while the jugulum is the ventral or underside. Laterally, between the nape and jugulum, are the two sides.

Although the two terms are used interchangeably, the operculum of a rock dove (right) overlaps the nostrils and is softer than the cere of a hawk (above), which is nearly as hard as the bill.

TWO

Skeletal Structure

The skeletal system of all birds has two distinctive characteristics. First, the bones throughout contain many air cavities and are said to be *pneumatized.* This type of bone structure is very lightweight and an asset to flight. Secondly, adjacent bones have a tendency to fuse together, thus appearing as one bone. This fusion of bones is especially noticeable in the skull of a bird.

Where two or more bones meet is called a joint, and if these bones move with respect to each other it is an articu-lated joint. Where two or more bones meet but do not move with respect to each other is known as a suture. The only articulated joints in the head of a bird are those of the mandible and the joint between the head and neck. All other joints of the head are either sutures or fusion processes.

The skull of a bird is very lightweight, containing many air cavities. The bones of the head include all the bones forward of the cervical vertebrae, which make up the neck of a bird.

The skeletal system of the head and neck of a crow. During normal stance, the neck has a natural S curve.

There are about three dozen separate bones that make up the head of a bird, but it is not necessary for the carver or artist to learn all these bones. What is important is to know and understand how these bones relate to the overall structure of the head, what parts a bird is capable of moving, and what happens when these parts move.

All the bones of the head that encapsulate the brain and form the basic structure of the face are collectively called the skull. In an adult bird, many bones of the skull have fused together so that they appear to be only one bone. Only a few bones of the head are moveable, with the lower mandible having the greatest amount of articulation.

There are more than nine thousand different species of birds recorded, and it is readily understandable that there are just as many different sizes and shapes of heads. Ornithologists use these differences, especially the differences of the bill, in order to help classify a species.

Although similar in structure, skull shapes vary considerably in different species primarily by the shape of the bill; the jay has a bill that is well adapted for eating a variety of foods, such as seeds, insects, worms, or dead animals.

The gull has a long bill that is hooked at the tip. This feature is ideal for catching and tearing apart the fish that gulls eat.

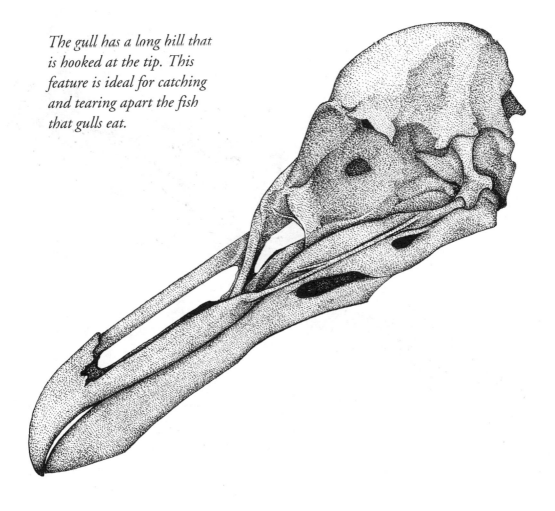

The cormorant has a bill that is long and slender with a sharp hook at the tip. The streamlined configuration of the bill and head, along with the hook, helps the bird catch fish as it dives underwater.

The skull can be divided into three basic parts, each containing specific bones or pairs of bones. The cranium is the bone structure forming the brain cavity and is made up of several separate bones that are fused together in an adult bird. In a hatchling bird these individual bones are readily visible and distinctively separate.

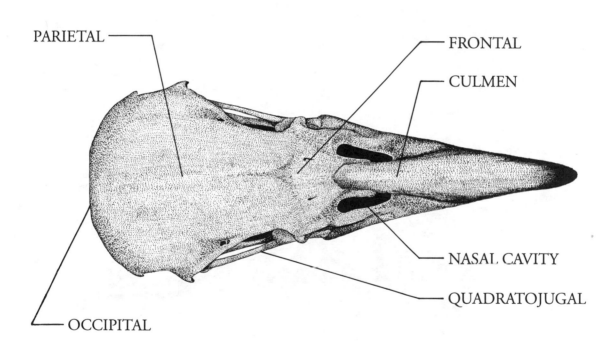

PARIETAL

FRONTAL

CULMEN

NASAL CAVITY

QUADRATOJUGAL

OCCIPITAL

Top view of a crow's skull showing the primary bones.

At the posterior (rear) of the skull is the occipital, which has on the ventral (under) side a ball-like projection called the occipital condoyle. This projection forms an articulated, or movable, joint with the uppermost end, or atlas, of the neck.

The parietals are a pair of bones, left and right, that cover the front portion of the brain cavity and form the base for the forehead, while the frontals are the bones that create the forehead. Squamosals, one on each side of the head, are located just below the orbit, or eye cavity, and complete the roof of the cranium. The lowermost point of each squamosal has a depression that is the socket of an articu-

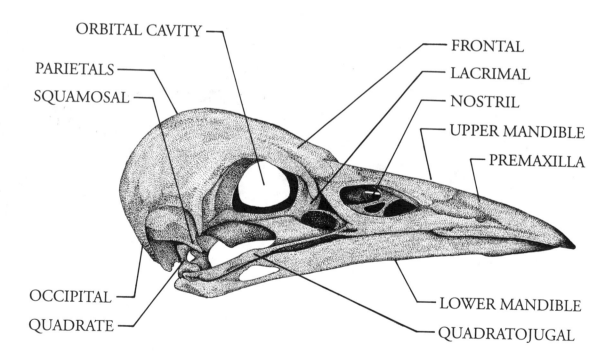

ORBITAL CAVITY
PARIETALS
SQUAMOSAL
FRONTAL
LACRIMAL
NOSTRIL
UPPER MANDIBLE
PREMAXILLA
OCCIPITAL
QUADRATE
LOWER MANDIBLE
QUADRATOJUGAL

Side view of a crow's skull showing the primary bones.

lated jointure with the quadrate bone. The sphenoid is the bone that forms the floor of the brain cavity.

A second group of bones are those of the face, which primarily make up the skeleton of the upper and lower mandible. The upper mandible is made up of many separate bones that have fused into one structure called the maxilla. The maxillae (plural) are the two primary bones of the upper mandible and are the left and right halves. These two halves are fused along their centerline to form the culmen.

The upper mandible is attached to the frontal by a movable hinge. This hinge allows the upper mandible to articulate slightly with the skull by a process called cranial kinesis. Kinesis is a process by which a joint articulates due to externally applied forces rather than by muscle force. Of the bill, this occurs during biting, eating, pecking, and swallowing food. The amount of movement varies between species depending upon their feeding habits. In fruit-eating birds, such as parrots, the movement is very pronounced, but it is greatly reduced in the ostrich, which must bite off the grasses it eats.

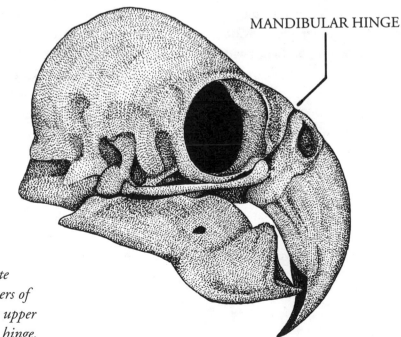

MANDIBULAR HINGE

Cranial kinesis is quite pronounced in members of the parrot family; the upper mandible moves on a hinge.

The nasals are a pair of bones that form the left and right nasal cavities. The lacrimals are a pair of bones, one on each side of the face, located at the front of each orbit and become the foundation of the lore. The lore on nearly all species is rather concave shaped, thus providing a sight channel for the eye. If the lore did not have this hollow shape, it would block the line of forward vision of the eye. On most passerines and waterfowl this sight channel extends to the rear of the eye, providing better protective vision.

The lower mandible is made up of ten separate bones (five on each side) that are fused into one rigid, V-shaped structure. On a few species, and on most very young birds, these bones are movable with respect to each other and provide the ability for the lower mandible to widen as the mouth is opened. This allows for the intake of larger pieces of food that the bird could otherwise not eat.

The posterior ends of the forked lower mandible form an articulated joint with the lower ends of the two quadrate bones. This joint becomes the angle-of-the-jaw. The quadrates are somewhat quadrangular in shape (thus the name), with four points of attachment. The lower, outermost point of the quadrate forms a joint with the quadratojugal. The quadratojugals are a pair of thin bones extending from each side of the upper mandible and are part of what is called the zygomatic bar.

The third group of bones in the head are those of the tongue and mouth. All the bones of the tongue collectively form the hyoid apparatus. The hyoid apparatus of the woodpecker is highly developed and along with the attached muscles becomes a mechanism that allows extreme extension and retraction of the tongue. With this ability the woodpecker can collect insects in the holes that are pecked in trees.

The orbital cavities are the sockets in the skull for the eyes. They are rather large and spacious and are separated from each other, along the midline of the skull, by a thin platelike bone called the interorbital septum. In hawks and eagles, there is additional cartilage, on the bone, above the orbital cavity. This gives the eyes a deep-set appearance and also alters the overall shape of the head.

Part of the skeletal system of the orbital region is the sclerotic ring. These small platelike bones are actually a part of the eye itself and are discussed more fully in chapter 6.

The sclerotic ring is a circle of small, over-lapping, platelike bones around the eye.

The neck of a bird is, in reality, an extension of the vertebral column, or backbone. The cervical vertebrae are the bones that make up the skeleton of the neck and are collectively called the cervical column. The cervical column extends from the skull to the first vertebra that is connected to the sternum (breastbone). The vertebrae of all birds and animals are homologous, or similar in structure, but in birds the cervical vertebrae have some different characteristics.

Humans, and most other mammals, have seven vertebrae in the neck, but birds have a varying number. Most passerines (perching birds) have thirteen or fourteen vertebrae while long-necked birds, such as cranes and egrets, have as many as twenty-five.

The cervical column is not a straight line, as might be suggested by the external appearance. The skeletal system of the neck has a conspicuous S-shaped curve during normal stance but can be stretched, straightened, or rotated during activities such as preening, sleeping, or displaying. This natural S curve of the neck skeleton, along with the bib feathers, produces a bulge in the jugulum region, just above the breast, which can be emphasized in a carving.

The first vertebra of the neck (closest to the head) is called the atlas. The ring-like shape of the atlas is the socket for a ball-and-socket joint with the occipital condoyle located at the base of the skull. The second cervical vertebra is called the axis, which becomes a platform upon which the atlas rotates as the head is turned. All the vertebrae of the neck form articulated joints with each other and their shape determines the extent of articulation. Due to the high number of vertebrae, a bird has much greater flexibility of the neck and head than a human does.

The skeleton of a duck's neck takes on an extreme S-curved shape when the bird is resting. This creates an additional bulge in the area above the breast.

THREE

Muscles

Muscles are the motor mechanisms that enable a bird or animal to move its skeletal structure, thus performing necessary functions such as walking, flying, eating, and so on. There are more than 175 different muscles on a bird, most of which are paired, or found on both the left and right side. The muscle mass makes up about two-thirds of the total weight of a bird.

Until 1979, when the International Committee on Avian Anatomical Nomenclature prepared the *Nomina Anatomica Avium*, a document suggesting that a common terminology be used, most ornithologists supplied names for muscles of their own liking or followed a predecessor's terminology. This committee suggested a list of muscle names that would be universally understood in a common language—Latin.

Unfortunately, most carvers and artists are not adequately versed in the Latin language and often have difficulty understanding muscle names. Learning about the muscles is somewhat easier if you understand how or why a muscle is given a particular name. A flexor, for example, is a muscle that causes a joint to lessen its angle, or flex, while an extensor is the companion muscle that causes the joint to straighten. Pairs of muscles are also named as to their size, such as longus and brevis (long and short) or magnus and minimus (large and small).

There are only a few muscles of the head and neck that are of much importance to the carver. Mainly, the muscles of the jaw are of primary importance. These muscles are the ones that allow the bird to open and close its mouth and to eat. Another set of muscles are those of the tongue. Although not critically important to the carver, they are an interesting subject, especially in the woodpecker.

Dependant upon the feeding methods, the muscles of the jaw vary considerably between species. Birds that generally swallow large pieces of food, such as hawks, owls, and eagles, have rather well-developed muscles that open the jaw. Birds that probe the ground with their bill or pry bark off trees in search of food also have relatively large muscles to open the jaw. Species that eat small insects or nectar have small and weak jaw muscles, and birds that have a loud or complex song have well-developed muscles of the syrinx or voice box. Birds that break open seeds and fruit or tear apart large prey have strong, well-developed muscles that close the jaw.

Muscles that open the jaw are larger and more fully developed in birds that eat large pieces of food.

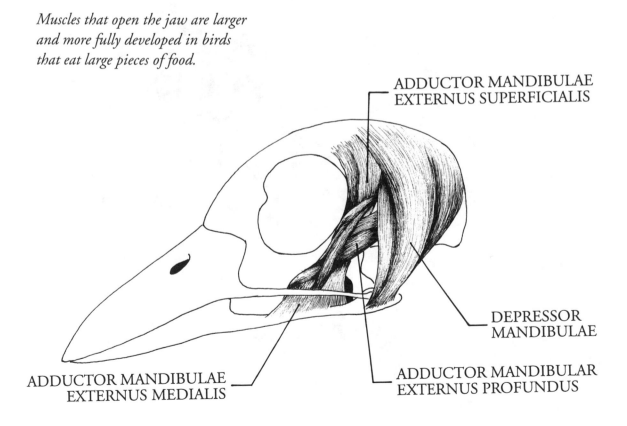

ADDUCTOR MANDIBULAE
EXTERNUS SUPERFICIALIS

DEPRESSOR
MANDIBULAE

ADDUCTOR MANDIBULAE
EXTERNUS MEDIALIS

ADDUCTOR MANDIBULAR
EXTERNUS PROFUNDUS

Birds that bite their food have stronger muscles that close the jaw.

ADDUCTOR MANDIBULAE
EXTERNUS SUPERFICIALIS

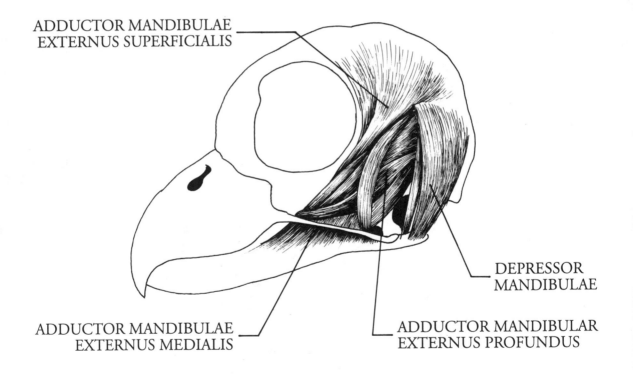

DEPRESSOR
MANDIBULAE

ADDUCTOR MANDIBULAE
EXTERNUS MEDIALIS

ADDUCTOR MANDIBULAR
EXTERNUS PROFUNDUS

The location and size of the jaw muscles clearly indicate one reason why the head has a puffed, "cheeky" appearance just below the eye. In most birds of prey, this "cheek" is often more pronounced than in small songbirds due to the fact that the muscles in birds of prey are larger and more highly developed.

The muscles of the neck are highly complex and well developed, especially in species that feed on active, fast-moving prey. Species with extremely long necks, such as egrets and cranes, have unusually well-developed and complex neck muscles. Generally, the muscles of the neck follow the basic skeletal shape, but in many species, the muscle that attaches the head to the neck is greatly enlarged just before hatching. This hatching muscle is used to help the chick break the eggshell with its bill.

Many long-necked birds, such as egrets, have a distinctive bend or kink in the neck about midpoint. The muscles surrounding this kink are more fully developed and allow the bird to move its head forward with a whiplike action when catching the fish that makes up most of its diet.

To gain a full appreciation of the complexity of the neck muscles, you simply need to watch the activity of a bird during preening, eating, or courtship rituals. A bird can manipulate its neck in order to place its head and bill in various locations about the body. A bird has the ability to reach nearly every part of its body with its bill, which becomes a tool for preening or scratching.

When resting or sleeping, many ducks will turn their heads to rest their chins on their backs with their bills tucked under the scapular feathers of a wing. At other times, a duck will simply lay its head upon its back with the bill resting on the neck, while looking straight ahead. This position causes the neck to take on an extreme curve, giving a fuller appearance to the breast.

Due to the complexity of the skeletomuscular system of the neck, a bird can manipulate its head into numerous positions—many times creating an awkward appearance. Often it is this head position that portrays the essence of the species, and a thorough study with good reference material is mandatory before carving any species.

FOUR

Covering

Encapsulating the skeleto-muscular structure of all birds and animals is a protective covering called the integument. The integument consists of the skin, hair, scales, and feathers. Compared to most other vertebrates, the skin of a bird is quite thin. It is made up of two layers: the dermis, or underlayer, and the epidermis, or surface layer. Visible on the surface of the epidermis are the feather follicles, or the points from which the feathers emerge through the skin.

The primary function of the skin is to protect the flesh and muscle beneath, but it serves many other purposes. Contained in the skin are smooth muscles, blood vessels, nerves, keratin, fatty tissue, and, in some cases, oil glands. A thin layer of tissue called facia joins the skin to the muscle underneath.

The skin of a bird is fitted quite loosely about the neck and rather tightly about the head. This loose fit of the skin in the neck area allows for extreme movement, which does not occur on the head. On a plucked bird, the ample neck skin often can be seen to have folds until the neck has been stretched or rotated, and the skin then becomes more taut.

Each feather on a bird grows from a feather follicle, which has a system of smooth muscles attached to it. This muscle system allows the bird to move its feathers, normally in a group, in order to help regulate body temperature, strike a threatening pose, or produce a mating display. In cold temperatures a bird will elevate, or "fluff," its feathers to create many insulating air pockets. In times of extreme heat, the bird will compress these groups of feathers, close to the body, which allows body heat to escape faster. A bird can also rotate, or twist, the feathers in a group.

The blood vessels contained in the skin are part of what gives the skin its color and sometimes the ability to change color. On certain species there are apteria, or featherless areas, that are often brightly colored. On the neck of a male sage grouse, for example, is a brightly colored apteria that inflates, with the use of an air sac, during mating rituals. The male ring-necked pheasant has a crimson orbital region that is nearly void of feathers. Due to increased blood flow, this orbital region becomes a much brighter red color during mating displays.

During a courtship display, the male sage grouse inflates air sacs to expose brightly colored patches of skin.

The part of the integument that covers the bill is called the ramphotheca. In most cases this is a very hard, durable, horny sheath made up mostly of keratin, which is the same protein substance that produces fingernails and hair in humans. Because of particular feeding habits, in a few species the ramphotheca is softer and more flexible. The upper mandible of the woodcock, for example, is somewhat flexible at the tip and is an aid when probing the soft earth in search of worms.

Also part of the ramphotheca is a horny, platelike projection that extends from the base of the upper mandible upward, covering the forehead. This frontal shield is seen in coots, swans, and gallinules and is often mistakenly thought of as being an enlarged or oversized upper mandible.

Contained in the integument are Herbst corpuscles, which are believed to give a bird a high sensitivity of touch. The bills of skimmers, for example, contain great numbers of Herbst corpuscles. As a skimmer flies with its lower mandible plowing the water, it can "feel" instantly when it is in contact with a fish and snap it up without hesitation.

FIVE

Bills

When describing the head of a bird, one cannot omit the bill as a major topic. The bill, or ramus, is in many cases the most distinctive feature of a bird's head and often the only part by which we recognize a particular species. The bill is a bone modification of the skull that is covered with a durable horny sheath, the ramphotheca, which is rather hard and rigid. Comprised of the upper and lower mandibles, the bill is basically a two-part structure. The cutting edges of the mandibles are called the tomia, and the fleshy corners of the mouth are called the rictus.

Prominent on ducks and geese is a hard protruding tip on the upper mandible called the nail. On very young ducklings, there is also a nail tooth. This is also located at the very tip of the upper mandible, toward the ventral side, and is used for pecking open the eggshell when hatching. As the duckling grows this nail tooth disappears or wears away, usually in a few days.

Ornithologists classify the bill of a bird into more than twenty different categories. It is not necessary that the carver learn all these categories, but it should indicate the importance of having good reference materials before starting a carving.

The nail tooth of a duckling disappears within a few days after hatching.

Bill shapes are categorized primarily by their external shape, structure, features, or size and are usually referenced to the features of the upper mandible. The bill of a green heron, for example, is markedly longer than the head and is classified as long, whereas the short bill is shorter than the head, as seen in the junco.

A long bill is considerably longer than the head, whereas the short bill is much shorter than the head, as seen in the green heron (above) and junco (right).

The upper mandible of hawks is longer than the lower mandible and curves at the tip to form the hooked bill. Sometimes the tips of the mandibles overlap each other like a pair of scissors and are classed as crossed, as in the crossbill. When the upper mandible is higher than it is wide, as in the puffin, it is said to be compressed, whereas a depressed mandible is wider than it is high, as seen on most ducks.

The upper mandible of a hawk is longer than the lower mandible and curves down at the tip creating the hooked bill.

When the mandibles overlap like a pair of shears, the bill is termed crossed, as in the crossbill.

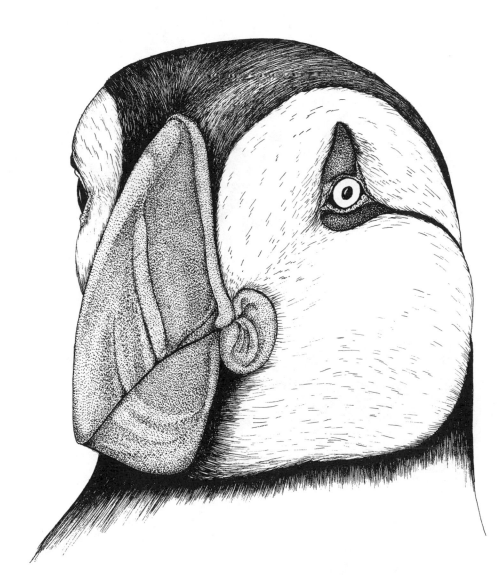

The bill of a puffin is obviously higher than it is wide and is called compressed.

A bill that is wider than it is high, such as a duck's, is called depressed.

The grouse and grosbeak have bills that are obviously high and wide, which are termed stout. The terete bill of a hummingbird has a cross-sectional shape that is round. When the commissure is in line with the head, the bill is said to be straight, as in the bittern. A bill is considered decurved if the tip curves downward, and recurved if the tip curves upward, as seen in the ibis and avocet respectively.

An ibis has a decurved bill.

The long bill of an avocet curves upward and is termed recurved.

The bill of a flamingo is deflected at a downward angle, near the midpoint of its length, and is said to be bent. A tanager has a mandible with convex sides and is classed as swollen, while the acute bill of the yellow warbler comes to a very sharp point. The tip of the hairy woodpecker's bill is beveled and is classed as chisel-like.

The flamingo has a bent bill with an obvious bend at the midpoint of the mandible.

The bill of a hairy wood-pecker, which has a beveled tip, is called chisel-like.

On a few species, the upper mandible has an obvious hump, as seen on the scoter, and is termed gibbous. The northern shoveler and the roseated spoonbill have a bill that is depressed and widened near the tip. This is the spatulate or spoon-shaped bill.

The scoter's bill has a distinct hump and is called gibbous.

The spoonbill has a
spatulate bill.

Birds have evolved dramatically since the time of Archeopteryx and no longer have teeth, but some species have what could be construed as teeth. Along the tomia, or cutting edges, on the mandibles of some species are lateral serrations, or toothlike ridges. Ducks, geese, and swans have these "teeth" and are said to have a bill that is lamellate, or sieve-billed.

When the tomia has a toothlike nick, usually near the tip, the bill is classed as notched. This notch usually occurs on the upper mandible, as seen in falcons. (Hawks do not have this notch.) Another shape is the conical, where the bill is quite short and cone shaped, as in the redpoll.

The notched bill of a falcon has a notch or tooth near the tip of the upper mandible.

There are several other external characteristics of the bill that help an ornithologist to catalogue or classify a species. The bill with an angulated commissure has a commissure line that is bent at the point where the tomia meets the rictus, as seen in grosbeaks and finches. Pelicans and cormorants have a bill with a gular sac. In pelicans, this is a conspicuous, unfeathered, fleshy sac or pouch on the ventral side of the lower mandible in the gular region. In the cormorant it is not so conspicuous and is partially feathered.

Variations of the nostrils also play an

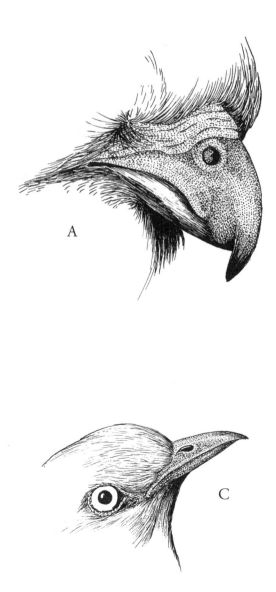

A

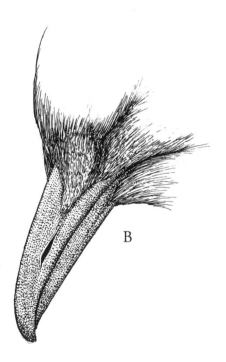

Nares, or nasal openings, appear in three basic shapes: circular (A), linear (B), and oval or teardrop (C).

B

C

important role when an ornithologist cata-logues a species. The nostrils of a bird are usually separated from each other by a bony wall called the nasal septum and are referred to as being imperforate. In some species, such as cranes and vultures, the nostrils do not have a nasal septum. Because you can literally see through the nostrils, in one and out the other, they are called perforate.

The common pigeon has a fleshy operculum that extends over the nostril openings. This operculate characteristic of the nostrils is apparent also in most hawks and falcons. Normally the operculum is fleshy and softer than the surrounding ramphotheca, but in some species it is membranous and nearly as hard as the bill itself, as seen in the barn swallow.

The shape of the nares, or nostril openings, are also a determining factor when classifying a species. The nares of a gull are linear in shape, forming a narrow slitlike opening, while accipiters, such as hawks and kites, have an oval, or teardrop-shaped nostril opening. Falcons have a cir-cular, or rounded, nostril opening. Members of the shearwater family have on each side of the upper mandible a hard tubelike structure that leads into the nos-trils. Members of this family and alba-trosses, which also have this special feature, are known as tubenoses.

Members of the shearwater or tubenose family have a tubular structure for the nasal passage, as seen in the storm petrel.

SIX

Eyes and Vision

The eyes of a bird are a highly specialized pair of organs that occupy the hollow spaces of the orbital cavities. Often larger and weighing more than the brain, the eyes make up a large percentage of the head, though only a small portion is visible on the surface. The eye of a bird differs from that of the human eye, and the eyes of other mammals, in three ways.

The overall shape differs by being pear-shaped or turnip-shaped rather than spherical, as in most mammals. There are six muscles attached to the eye, but a bird generally has little or no movement of the eye. The eye is more or less fixed in the socket, and birds must turn their head and neck to look in different directions. Owls cannot move their eyes at all but compensate for this by being able to rotate their heads more than 180 degrees.

Visible on the surface of the eye is only the black pupil and the iris, or colored part, of the eye. The pupil is actually an aperture or a round hole in the iris that allows light to pass through. Skimmers are the exception to this pupil shape. Instead of being round, the pupil of a skimmer's eye is a vertical catlike slit. Also, the king penguin can contract its pupil to a small square.

The iris is what gives the eye its distinctive color. Eye color is accomplished by the presence of pigments, melanins, or colored oils in the eye. Pigments and melanins produce a specific color, such as yellow, red, or brown, while colored oils create the appearance of silver, gold, or other metallic colors. Another way the iris appears to have a particular color is by light interference. Often the eye gets its color from a combination of these two methods.

Generally, in passerines, the iris is a dark brown color but could be yellow, red, or some other color. Most owls have yellow eyes, as do many hawks, and there can be color differences between the sexes of the same species. Young or immature birds often have a different eye color than their adult counterparts. The immature redtail hawk, for example, has yellowish eyes that become a reddish-brown after the first year. Due to the absence of pigments in albino birds, the iris is normally red or pink. This reddish color is achieved from the red blood cells present in the eye.

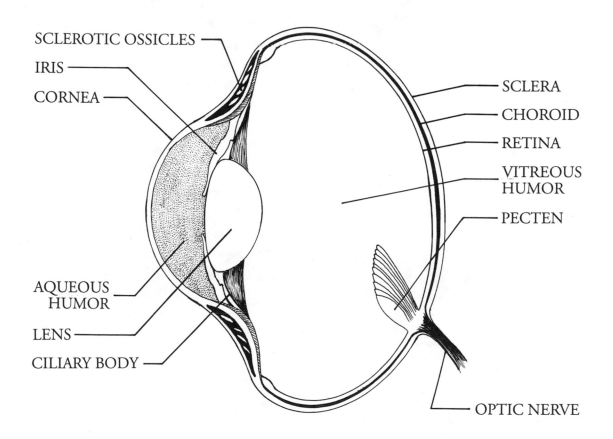

SCLEROTIC OSSICLES

IRIS

CORNEA

SCLERA

CHOROID

RETINA

VITREOUS HUMOR

PECTEN

AQUEOUS HUMOR

LENS

CILIARY BODY

OPTIC NERVE

The various parts of a bird's eye. Nutrients are supplied to the eye by the pleated structure of the pecten.

Covering the entire front surface of the eye is a transparent membrane—the cornea. Behind the cornea is a fluid filled cavity called the aqueous humor. The pupil, or opening in the center of the iris, can vary in diameter depending upon the amount of light present. It is for this reason that nocturnal birds such as owls, which are active during dim light, tend to have rather large pupils relative to the overall size of the eye. Diurnal, or daytime birds, generally have a proportionately smaller pupil.

The purpose of the lens is exactly as its name implies: to focus the visual image.

The lens is held in place, and also focused, by the ciliary body. Focusing is accomplished by changing the surface shape of the lens through an action called accommodation. In most birds, this accommodation takes place by changing the curvature of the lens. The lens is flattened to view distant objects and more curved to view nearer objects. The distance, or range, to which accommodation will focus the eye is expressed in diopters. A diopter is the reciprocal number of the focal length, expressed in meters. For example, a lens of one diopter will focus on an object one

A bird's visual acuity is about ten times better than that of humans. A hawk would be able to see details of a dormouse much more clearly than a human would.

meter away (and beyond), while a lens of two diopters will focus at a distance of one-half meter (1 ÷ 2 = $^1/_2$), and beyond.

Humans have a lens of about ten diopters, owls vary from two to four, and most land birds have from eight to twelve diopter lenses. Aquatic birds, such as cormorants, have a focal range of about forty to fifty diopters. A few birds are myopic, or nearsighted, under certain conditions. When out of the water, penguins do not see very well and kiwis can barely see anything during the daytime unless the object is very close to them.

The eyes of hawks and eagles have a highly developed system of accommodation because not only is the lens focused but to some extent the cornea is too. Focusing of the cornea is not done in the human eye or any other mammal. By changing the curvature of both the cornea and the lens, the eye can focus very rapidly, from quite near to very far vision, during pursuit of fast-moving prey.

The rear wall of the eye is made up of three layers. The outer layer is the sclera, the middle layer is the choroid, and the inner layer is the retina. The eye functions

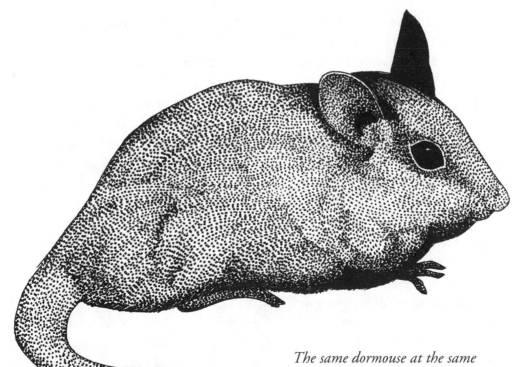

The same dormouse at the same distance would look less clear to a human.

much like a simple camera. Light enters the pupil, passes through the lens, and a visual image is cast upon the retina. It is the retina that is the "film" or "image screen." The image on the retina is transferred to the brain via the optic nerve.

The retina contains rods and cones, which are the receptor cells that transfer the visual image to the optic nerve. The rods are most effective in dim light, and cones function best in bright light. Diurnal, or daytime, birds have an abundance of cones, whereas nocturnal birds, such as owls, have many more rods. The cones are sparsely distributed over the retina in all birds, except in spots called foveae. A fovea contains high concentrations of cones to give points of sharpest vision. Hawks, and other birds of prey, have two foveae in each eye, giving them the ability to triangulate their field of vision, thus being able to pinpoint the exact location and distance to their prey.

In each human fovea, there are about 200,000 visual cells per square millimeter whereas the buzzard, with an eye about the same size as man, has in each fovea about one million cells per square millimeter. This would indicate that a buzzard has a visual acuity of about five times better than man. Visual acuity refers to the ability of the eye to focus clearly and sharply on an object as it becomes smaller, or more distant.

Nocturnal, or night-active, birds have an abundance of rods in the retina of the eye. Rods are particularly sensitive in dim light due to a purple-red pigment called rhodopsin, or visual purple, which contains a protein and a derivative of vitamin A. When bright light reaches the rhodopsin, the two main components are "bleached" or separated. This results in reducing or totally destroying the response to light waves. In dim light or darkness, however, the protein and vitamin derivative combine by synthesis, thus increasing retinal sensitivity.

The third difference of the eye is the manner in which the eye receives nutrients. In mammals, the eyes are supplied with nutrients and oxygen through a system of blood vessels on the surface of the retina, but in birds, this function is accomplished by a structure called the pecten. The pecten structure is found on the inner surface of the retina and protrudes into the vitreous humor, or chamber. Nutrients are diffused from its rippled, or pleated, surface to feed the eye. The size of the pecten varies greatly between species, and ornithologists cannot quite agree on the reason for this.

The sclerotic ring, mentioned earlier, is a bone structure around the perimeter on the front of the eye. It is made up of many tiny platelike bones, which collectively are termed the scleral ossicles. The sclerotic ring is held in place by the sclera, or outer layer, of the eye wall.

There is a great amount of variety between species, in eye size, color, eye position, and visual field. The visual field is generally divided into two types of vision: binocular and monocular. Binocular vision is the area that a bird sees with both eyes while monocular vision is that area seen with only one eye. Owls, with their eyes placed forward, have monocular vision of about 60–70 degrees and binocular vision of about the same area. This relatively narrow field of vision receives compensation by an owl's ability to rotate its head in nearly a full circle.

An owl has monocular vision of 65–70 degrees and binocular vision over most of the same area.

In extreme opposition to an owl's narrow visual field is the visual field of the woodcock. With the eyes set high, far back, and on the sides of the head, a woodcock has monocular vision of more than 180 degrees with a narrow line of binocular vision. There is very little blind area and therefore a good defensive vision for protection.

Generally, birds of prey (hawks, owls, eagles) have eyes that are placed for forward vision while nearly all other birds have their eyes set more toward the sides of the head for better protective vision. This is generally true even in mammals where the prey (mice or rabbits, for example) have eyes set for wide vision and the predators (cats, foxes, and so on) have forward-set eyes.

With eyes set high and far back on the head, the woodcock has monocular vision of more than 180 degrees but very limited binocular vision.

The bittern, however, has an unusual eye placement that is low and downward to aid in the search of food with its long bill. When alarmed or threatened, the bittern will sit motionless with its bill pointed skyward. This has a twofold purpose: It allows for more protective forward vision, and at the same time it provides some degree of camouflage because the bittern's bill tends to resemble the reeds and grasses of the surrounding normal habitat.

The bittern, with eyes set for downward vision, will often sit motionless with the bill pointed upward as a means of protection.

Each species has a definite set to the eyes, and good reference material is necessary if you want your carving to be accurate. Photographs of a bird's head are a very good source of reference. Measurements can be taken from the photos and transferred to the carving. Several measurements should be considered for accuracy, which is explained in chapter 7.

Do birds see in color or monochrome shades of gray? Until recently, this question was a source of considerable debate among ornithologists. Recent studies and experiments have proven that certain species such as ducks, owls, passerines, and hummingbirds have the ability to see color, and it is safe to assume that all birds see color to some extent.

Further evidence indicates that the mallard and the black-chinned hummingbird can see into the ultraviolet color spectrum—something that humans and other mammals cannot do. It is believed that such ultraviolet sensitivity aids the hummingbird in detecting flowers that strongly reflect ultraviolet light. The smooth skin of many fruits also reflect ultraviolet light more than the surrounding leaves. This could help fruit-eating birds to more easily detect their food.

Another part of the orbital region is the eyelids, both upper and lower, and the nictitating membrane. The upper and lower eyelids are simply folds of skin that cover the front surface of the eye. The nictitating membrane is a transparent tissue

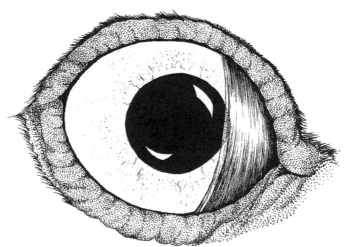

The nictitating membrane, or third eyelid, is used to clean, moisten, and protect the eye.

located just under the eyelids at the nasal canthus, or front corner of the eye. Tiny muscles connected to the eyelids allow the bird to open, close, or blink the lids when necessary. Blinking is a normal function of both mammals and birds. All birds blink and close their eyelids, but not all do so in the same manner.

Some birds blink only with the nictitating membrane while others blink only with the eyelids. Some species blink with both the eyelids and the nictitating membrane at the same time. Generally, in nocturnal (night active) birds the upper eyelid comes down farther than the lower eyelid travels upward. In diurnal (daytime) birds, the opposite is true. The lower eyelid comes up farther than the upper eyelid travels down. Unlike mammals, all birds close their eyes upon death.

The nictitating membrane, or "third eyelid" is used as a lens cleaner or dirt shield. When the nictitating membrane is drawn across the eye, it cleans the cornea of dirt and also spreads moisture that is secreted in the eye glands located beneath the membrane. On a windy day, a bird may close the nictitating membrane to protect the eye from blowing dust and dirt.

There are two types of eye glands found in the eye of a bird, and the eyes of all birds have both types. The lachrymal gland produces and secretes moisture, which the nictitating membrane spreads across the eye. Harderian glands are another type of lachrymal that were named for J. J. Harder, a Swiss anatomist. Harderians produce an oily secretion also used to moisten the eye. In marine birds, such as cormorants, the lachrymal glands are small compared to the Harderian glands, since these water birds require less moisture for the eye. The larger Harderians produce more oils to protect the eye from the effects of salt water.

In some species, such as the mallard duck, the eyelids are a distinctively different color than the surrounding area. This protective camouflage gives the appearance of a wide-open eye even when the lids are closed while the duck sleeps. During sleep, all birds will open one or both eyes for a few seconds to get a peek at the surroundings. If there is no disturbance, the eye is closed and sleep continues.

SEVEN

Measurement

Ornithologists, and most naturalists, take many measurements of a bird while gathering information about a species. These measurements are an aid in evaluating growth rate, sexual differences, and geographical size variations. Measurements are nearly always taken of the bill and are recorded on charts, usually in millimeters, under the heading of B (for bill).

The bill is measured from the tip of the upper mandible to the point where the bill joins the skull. This is always a straight-line measurement, even though the bill may be curved or hooked. When available, these measurements are a great asset to the carver and often are the first reference point in creating the head of a bird.

When carving the head of a bird (or painting a picture of one) several measurements should be taken to assure accuracy. Different carving techniques dictate the manner or sequence in the way the measurements are made, but one thing is certain—you must make measurements.

The bill (mandible) is always in-line right on the centerline of the head when viewed from above and never wider on one side than the other. Also, the distance from the tip of the mandible to each nostril is identical. The distance from the tip of the bill to the center of each eye must be the same. Another measurement consideration might be the distance from the top of the head to the center of the eye.

The bill is measured in a straight line even though the bill may be curved.

Some carvers prefer to drill the eye-holes into the blank cutout. By drilling all the way through the blank, they are assured that the holes are equally spaced on both sides of the head, provided of course that they carve both sides equally.

Other carvers will make the one eye socket slightly larger than necessary so they can adjust one eye to match the other. Whatever method is used, the important thing to remember is to measure.

Accurate measurement is critical in eye placement on a carving. One important measurement is the distance from the center of the eye to the tip of the bill.

*It is important to accurately
measure the distance from the
center of the eye to the top of
the head.*

Symmetry is not the only consideration, however, in placing the eyes. Different species have eyes set at different angles with respect to the centerline of the head. Each species has a definite set to its eyes and good reference photos are a must when making a carving.

The angle of eyeset is also a critical measurement when sculpting a bird.

Most carvers today use commercially produced glass eyes for their carvings rather than making their own because the process requires special materials, tools, and skills. However, this should not deter a carver from experimenting with different techniques. A handful of today's carvers do carve the eyes as an integral part of the head, directly in the wood, paint them to the desired color, then coat them with clear epoxy.

There are many different methods of setting glass eyes into the head of a carving. Most carvers use a puttylike, self-hardening substance rather than a glue. Compounds such as Plastic Wood, Plumber's Putty, two-part epoxies, and various others compounds are used for this purpose. Experimentation will help you decide which product you prefer. The eyelids and nictitating membrane can be formed with the same material used for installing the eyes.

When purchasing ready-made glass eyes, a carver should be careful to select the proper size and color for the species. Glass eyes used for carvings or taxidermy work are not the size of the total eye of a bird. Glass eyes are only the iris, or colored part, of the eye and the eye of a bird is much larger overall than the iris. Most supply houses have a comparative list of the correct size eye to use for the bird you are carving, but these lists are often compiled for taxidermists, who use eyes somewhat larger than does the carver. Eye sizes vary tremendously between species, and often there is a variation of size between sexes of the same species.

Large hawks and owls have an overall eye size about the same as humans, while the ostrich has the largest of all birds' eyes—about two inches in diameter. Charts I and II show the eye size and color for many species of birds, but these sizes could vary slightly depending upon the size of your carving.

Selecting the correct color and size of eye to use for your carving will play an important part in the final results. Since manufactured glass eyes are not totally consistent, you may have to compare several different eyes in order to get a matching pair with the same size pupils and the correct coloration.

EYE SIZE CHART I
Songbirds and Game Birds

SPECIES	MM	COLOR	SPECIES	MM	COLOR
Bittern	11	Yellow	Killdeer	7	Brown
Blackbird			Magpie	8	Brown
Redwing	5	Brown	Meadowlark	7	Brown
Rusty	5	Brown	Mockingbird	5	Brown
Brewers	6	Yellow	Mudhen	10	Red
Yellow Headed	6	Brown	Partridge	10	Hazel
Bluebird	4	Brown	Pelican		
Bluejay	7	Hazel	Brown	17	Straw
Bobolink	5	Brown	Pheasant (Cock)	10–11	Special
Bobwhite Quail	8	Hazel	Pheasant (Hen)	10–11	Brown
Bullfinch	6	Brown	Pigeon	8	Orange
Buzzard	12	Brown	Plover	6	Green
Cardinal	5	Brown	Prairie Chicken	10	Hazel
Catbird	5	Brown	Ptarmigan	9	Brown
Chickadee	4	Brown	Quail		
Chicken (Domestic)	10	Hazel	Bobwhite	8	Hazel
Cowbird	6	Brown	Rails		
Crane, Sandhill	12	Straw	Clapper	10	Hazel
Crossbill	5	Brown	Carolina	8	Red
Crow	11	Brown	Little Black	5	Brown
Cuckoo	7	Brown	King	9	Brown
Dove			Virginia	9	Hazel
Mourning	7	Brown	Yellow	6	Brown
Turtle	7	Brown	Roadrunner	10	Yellow
White-winged	8	Orange	Robin	6	Brown
Finches	4	Brown	Sandpiper	6–7	Brown
Flicker	8	Brown	Snipe	7	Brown
Grackle	5	Straw	Sparrow	3	Brown
Grouse			Starling	5	Brown
Ruffed	10	Hazel	Swallow	4	Brown
Sage	9	Hazel	Tern	6	Brown
Sharptail	9	Hazel	Thrush	6	Brown
Ptarmigan	7	Dark Brown	Turkey	12	Brown
Gull			Woodcock	8	Brown
Black-backed	14	Yellow	Woodpecker		
Bonaparte	9	Brown	Downy	5	Brown
Franklin	9	Brown	Flicker	8	Brown
Glaucus	14	Straw	Ivory-billed	12	Yellow
Herring	12	Yellow	Red-bellied	7	Red
Laughing	10	Red	Red-headed	6	Brown
Ring-billed	10	Yellow	White-headed	6	Red
Kingfisher, Belted	10	Brown			

EYE SIZE CHART II
Waterfowl and Birds of Prey

SPECIES	MM	COLOR	SPECIES	MM	COLOR
Duck			Widgeon	10	Brown
Bald Pate	9	Hazel	Wood Duck (Drake)	11	Red
Black	10	Dark Brown	Wood Duck (Hen)	11	Brown
Bufflehead	9	Brown			
Bluebill	10	Yellow	Eagle		
Canvasback (Drake)	10	Red	Bald (Adult)	17	Yellow
Canvasback (Hen)	10	Brown	Bald (Young)	16	Brown
Eider, Common	11	Brown	Golden	18	Brown
Eider, Spectacled	11	White			
Flordia	11	Brown	Falcon		
Gadwall	9	Brown	Perigrine	12	Brown
Goldeneye	11	Yellow	Kestrel	9	Brown
Harlequin	10	Brown			
Mallard	10	Brown	Goose		
Merganser			Brant	11	Brown
American (Drake)	10	Red	Canada	12	Brown
American (Hen)	10	Hazel			
Hooded (Drake)	9	Yellow	Hawk		
Hooded (Hen)	9	Hazel	Cooper	12	Straw
Redbreast (Drake)	10	Red	Fish (Osprey)	14	Yellow
Redbreast (Hen)	10	Hazel	Goshawk	14	Hazel
Old Squaw	9	Hazel	Marsh	12	Yellow
Pintail	9	Brown	Redtail	14	Brown
Red Head (Drake)	10	Dark Yellow	Rough Leg	14	Hazel
Redhead (Hen)	10	Brown	Red Shoulder	14	Hazel
Ring-necked (Drake)	9	Straw	Sharp-shinned	10	Yellow
Ring-necked (Hen)	9	Hazel	Swainsons	14	Hazel
Ruddy	10	Brown			
Scaup	9	Yellow	Owl		
Scoter			Arctic	20	Straw
Black	10	Brown	Barn	14	Brown
Common	10	Yellow	Barred	18	Special
Surf (Drake)	10	White	Burrowing	10	Yellow
Surf (Hen)	10	Brown	Elf	10	Yellow
Whitewinged	10	Straw	Great Horned	20	Yellow
Shoveler (Drake)	10	Yellow	Long-eared	14	Yellow
Spoonbill	10	Yellow	Pigmy	12	Yellow
Teal			Richardson	14	Straw
Bluewing	7	Brown	Screech	14	Straw
Cinnamon (Drake)	8	Dark Yellow	Sawhet	12	Straw
Cinnamon (Hen)	7	Brown	Snowy	18	Straw
Greenwing	8	Hazel	Short-eared	14	Yellow

EIGHT

Plumage

Several flightless species of birds, such as penguins, ostriches, and rheas, have their feathers distributed rather evenly over their bodies. This is not the typical arrangement on most birds. The majority of species have the feathers arranged in specific patterns and located in specific areas called tracts. Between the different tracts are featherless areas, or apteria. Areas where feathers grow are called pterylae (singular is pteryla). There are only two feather tracts on the head of a bird, and two on the neck.

The capital tract (pterylae capitalis) covers the area on top of the head, beginning at the base of the upper mandible and continuing rearward to the point where the head attaches to the neck. The side boundaries are an imaginary line from the angle of the jaw to the bottom of the occiput.

The second feather tract of the head is the ventral tract (pterylae ventralis), which begins on the ventral side of the lower mandible and continues all the way to the vent of the bird. As in the head, the neck also has only two feather tracts.

The dorsal, or top part of the neck contains the dorsal tract, (pterylae dorsalis), which extends from the atlas of the neck to the tail. The dorsal tract can be divided into several parts, and sometimes the area posterior to the nape is called the spinal tract (pterylae spinalis).

Feathers on the ventral, or underside of the neck lie in the aforementioned ventral tract, although some authorities refer to this area of the neck as the gular tract. On each side of the neck is a narrow apteria, or bald area, lying between the two feather tracts.

Within any feather tract there are regions, or feather groups. On the crown of some species is a group of longer, more erect feathers called the crest, as seen in cardinals and blue jays. Crests appear in several species, and in a variety of shapes and sizes. Even the feather types differ in crests of different species.

The crest of the California quail, for example, is a tuft of long, totally erect feathers that curl forward. The hooded merganser has a crest of spiny, bristlelike feathers that give the appearance of the bird wearing a hood. With the smooth muscles in the skin, all birds can raise the feathers of the crown, but birds that have a crest tend to have these feathers more erect at all times.

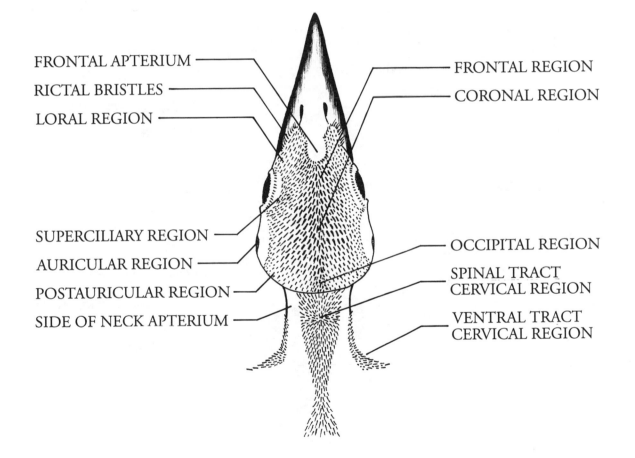

FRONTAL APTERIUM

RICTAL BRISTLES

LORAL REGION

SUPERCILIARY REGION

AURICULAR REGION

POSTAURICULAR REGION

SIDE OF NECK APTERIUM

FRONTAL REGION

CORONAL REGION

OCCIPITAL REGION

SPINAL TRACT
CERVICAL REGION

VENTRAL TRACT
CERVICAL REGION

There are but two feather tracts on the head, capital and ventral. The neck contains the dorsal and the ventral tracts. This is a dorsal view.

Similar to the crest is another conspicuous feather group found in herons and egrets. These birds, especially during mating season, have extremely long feathers growing from the crown and occiput that often drape down the neck. These plumes are a particular type of feather referred to in French as *aigrettes.* This is the basis for naming the species.

Covering the ear opening is the group of auriculars and just below, and forward, are the malars, or malar patch. Often these feathers of the malar patch are a distinctively different color and the bird is said to have a mustache. The chin contains a group of tiny feathers and the bib below is yet another group. In hummingbirds the bib is often iridescent, extending far to the sides, and is called the gorget.

The ventral view of the neck shows the ventral tract and feather regions

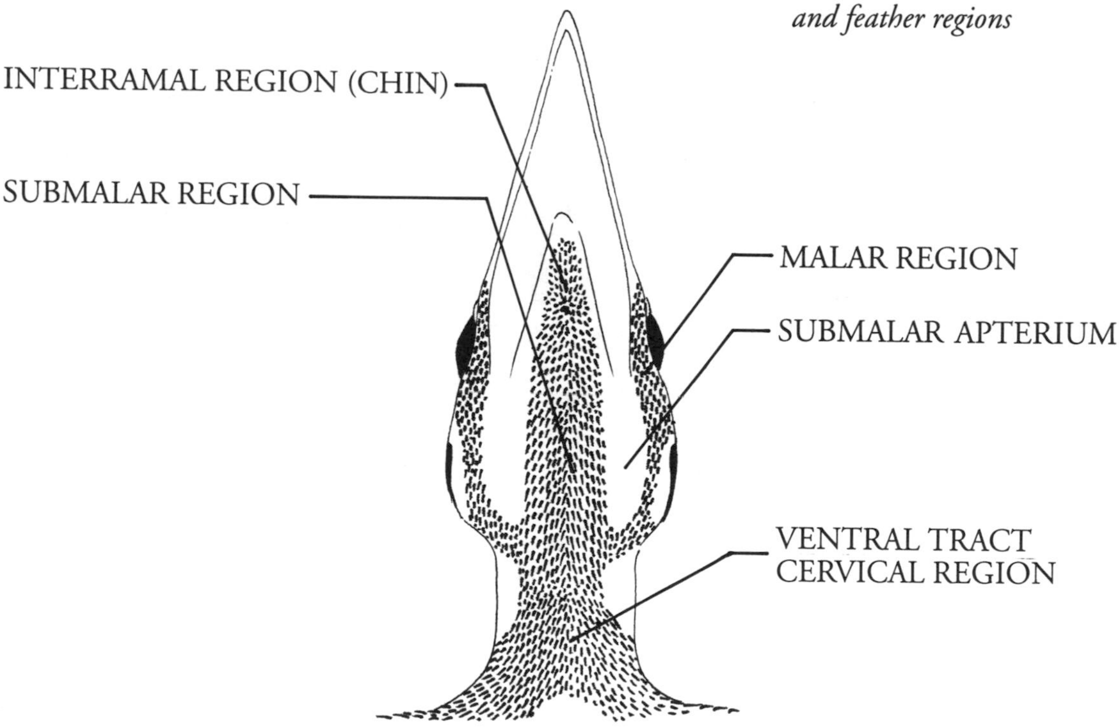

INTERRAMAL REGION (CHIN)

SUBMALAR REGION

MALAR REGION

SUBMALAR APTERIUM

VENTRAL TRACT CERVICAL REGION

The California quail has an erect plume of feathers on the forehead.

The eye-ring is the group of tiny feathers immediately surrounding the eye. In some species, the eye-ring is a different color than the remainder of the head. Following the superciliary line above the eye, there sometimes appears a streak of contrasting colored feathers (usually white) known as the eye stripe. The eye stripe appears in many species such as sandpipers, sparrows, wrens, and others.

In most owls, the orbital region is quite large and is covered by a circlet feather group called the facial disc. Also on some owls and other species is a group of longer, more erect feathers above the orbital region. These protruding, longer feathers are referred to as ear tufts, even though they are not associated with the ears. They simply look like a pair of ears on the bird and on some species resemble eyebrows. The eared grebe and the long-eared owl were named because of the long stringy feathers above the eye that resemble ears.

The ear tufts of the long-eared owl have no relationship to hearing; they simply look like ears.

The lores contain yet another group of feathers as does the nape. At the edge of the lore, next to the bill, is sometimes found long, whiskerlike feathers called bristles. These bristles are believed to be an aid for some species that catch insects in flight by acting as a net for the entrapment of the prey.

Whiskerlike bristles on the lore of a nightjar create a net to catch insects while the bird is flying in search of food.

Feather groups on a bird are often readily distinguished one from another either by color differences or by obvious differences in the size and shape of the feathers. The pteria and apteria (feathered and bald areas) vary somewhat between species, but the feather tracts and feather groups are very similar on nearly all species. In only a few species, such as the penguin, are the feathers spread evenly over the entire body.

COLORATION

The shape and size of the head is a primary means of identifying any species, but coloration is probably the most popular way of recognizing a species. Feathers receive their colors basically in two different ways. Chemical coloration is a method of feather coloration due to the presence of color pigments called biochromes, which account for the many different colors of birds in general. The second method of coloration is by structural coloration, which means that the feather structure, both surface and internal, reflects light in different manners. Iridescence is one form of structural coloration. Light is diffracted, or scattered, when it strikes the feather, producing a glowing and reflective appearance.

As mentioned earlier, the bib, malar patch, and eye-ring are usually a different color than the surrounding areas. So too is the eye stripe. The eye stripe is not seen on all species, but in those that have an eye stripe, it is always a different color than the surrounding feathers, thus giving the appearance of an eyebrow.

NINE

Special Features

Relevant to nearly any rule is, of course, the exception. In the case of a bird's head, there seem to be nearly as many exceptions as there are general rules. Head shape differs with each species even though the structure is basically the same. Size also has a wide range of variables, as does color, which often varies within a species by the age or sex of a bird. There are, however, some special head features among birds worth mentioning.

Bare, unfeathered areas are often seen on the head in several species, or, as in vultures, the head could be totally devoid of feathers. Some species have the additional growth of wattles, caruncles, or a comb.

Wattles are a flap, or pendant growth, of bare skin that hangs pendant-style from the head or, more specifically, from below the bill of certain species. Fleshy and usually brightly colored, wattles are of two types and appear in domestic chickens, turkeys, and some other members of gallinules.

One type of wattle hangs from the lower bill and is called a dewlap, or more commonly, a throat wattle. Another type of wattle is the lappet, which is a featherless, fleshy, flaplike extension of the rictus (fleshy corner of the mouth). Commonly called rictal wattles, these appear in the family Callaeidae (wattlebirds), and include species such as the wattled crow and the wattled starling. The wattle is a form of caruncle.

Caruncles are also naked, fleshy protuberances that have a wrinkled or warty appearance and are found on the head or upper neck area of a bird. On the wild turkey, they appear on the sides of the head and neck and also as a snood, or leader, which grows from the forehead and drapes over the upper bill.

On the head of the wild turkey are wattles, carun-cles, and a snood or leader.

Combs are yet another form of caruncle that grow on the top of the head. A comb differs from a snood in that it stands erect, instead of drooping, and has a serrated, toothlike edge, giving it the appearance, and thus its name, of a comb. Several species of grouse have a small comb over each eye. Similar to a frontal shield is the casque, which is a bony outgrowth on the crown and forehead, as seen in cassowaries and some hornbills.

On the crown of the domestic chicken is an erect fleshy outgrowth called a comb.

The horny growth on the crown and forehead of the cassowary is called a casque.

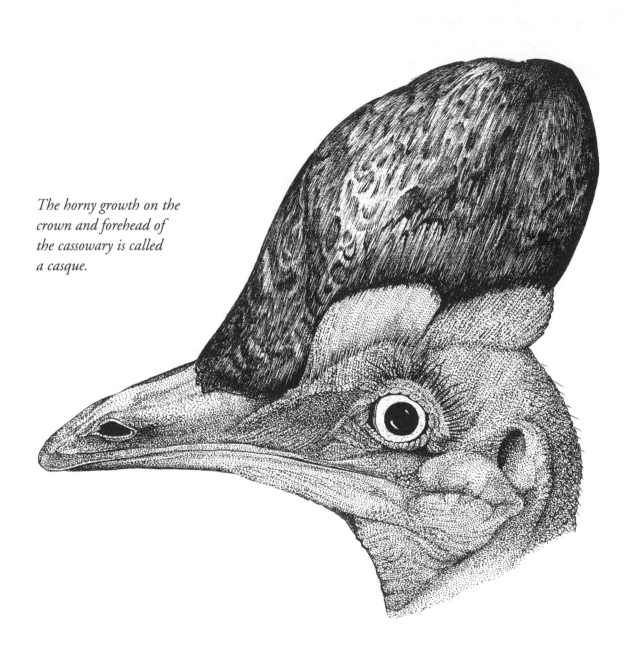

*The male frigatebird inflates
air sacs in the gular region to
create a bright colored bubble
during courtship display.*

Some species, during mating season, have peculiar growths about the head that disappear for the remainder of the year. Just before mating season, the male white pelican, for example, grows a hard protuberance on the upper mandible, which later disappears. This might be a way of protecting the fleshy gular sac from damage during fights with other males.

The orbital region of certain species often has some distinct special features. The male ring-necked pheasant has a brightly colored, featherless patch of exposed skin encircling the eye. The Atlantic puffin has a scaly area above and below the eye, while the lores of herons are void of feathers.

The respiratory (breathing) system of all birds has, in addition to lungs, several air sacs which are bladderlike bubbles located just under the skin. These sacs serve several purposes and functions related to the breathing of the bird. Of interest as a special feature is the air sacs of some members of the grouse family. The male sage grouse, for example, will inflate these air sacs during courtship rituals. The inflated sacs stretch the skin on the neck to expose apteria (bare) areas of the neck and create a brightly colored bubble in the gular region. The male frigate bird performs in a similar manner.

Although not visible on the surface, the ear openings of owls are different than most birds. Owls have one ear opening located higher on one side of the head than on the other, but the feathers covering the ears are symmetrically balanced on both sides of the head. Because owls hunt more by sound than by sight, this offset elevation of the ears may be a means of triangulating sound as an aid in locating prey.

Other special features, such as frontal shields, crests, and ceres, were described in previous chapters and will not be mentioned here. Of the approximately 9,600 recorded species, there are, perhaps, just as many variations or special features of the head. As new species are discovered, there surely will be many more.

TEN

Attitude and Position

When you create a carving or a painting of a bird, you should pay careful attention to the attitude or position of the head. Each species has definite head positions depending upon what the bird is doing. When a robin cocks its head as it hops about your lawn, it is doing so in search of food. Because the eyes are fixed in the sockets, the bird must cock its head to see down to the ground. An owl will sometimes turn its head upside-down in order to get a different view of what it is looking at.

Better vision is not the only reason, however, that a bird changes its head position. Some species of songbirds will tilt their heads upward while stretching their necks to emit their loud, clear songs. During rest or sleep many species will tuck their bills into the feathers of their lower necks while others will turn their heads to the rear and rest their bills on their backs. Certain species will bob their heads for-

ward and back while walking in order to maintain better balance.

During mating rituals, many species exhibit unusual head positions. The western grebe, for example, will point its bill skyward and stretch its long neck during a courtship ritual. Immediately after copulation, the grebe will lay its head far back over its dorsal region while spreading its wings upward.

The head attitude of most ducks usually determines the bird's disposition. When a duck is frightened or cautious, the bird will hold its head high for better visibility, and when it relaxes, the head is held low and close to the body.

When flying, all birds keep their heads perpendicular to the ground, thus keeping the eyes parallel to the horizon even if the body is banked in a turn. When flying, early aviators used this same method of horizon reference in order to keep their planes straight and level.

ELEVEN

Learning More

Someone once said that know-how is 90 percent "know" and 10 percent "how." This holds true with carving or painting a picture of a wildfowl. The more you know about your subject, the easier it is to depict it more accurately. For any artist, getting the "know" is a never-ending process that requires the use of many different sources.

Whatever methods you use to learn more about birds, it can safely be assumed that you will never acquire all the information known today about birds. Like a skilled surgeon, carvers or artists can improve their ability with practice, but they must also continue to learn more about the subject matter.

Although there is much information given (both technically and artistically) in this volume, it would require many volumes to compile the known information about the heads of all birds. It might be safe to assume that any single species could fill a volume with pertinent information. However, as much general information as possible that may be useful to the carver and artist has been submitted here.

In doing so, some points that some artisans may deem important undoubtedly have been omitted. Some omissions were deliberate since these items will appear in future volumes of the *Birds* series, while others were mere oversights that hopefully will be included in later volumes.

Knowing the anatomy and structure of the head can be a great asset when producing a carving or painting of a bird. The availability of study skins or taxidermy mounts is also an invaluable aid. With a study skin or mount, many measurements should be made to ensure accuracy of the carving. As stated before, the head truly conveys the essence of the species and should be the one part of bird anatomy that gets extra attention.

When we look at the face of a human, we many times create in our minds a stereotyped character portrait of the person. This is also true when we observe the head of a bird. With deep-set, forward-angled eyes, an eagle or hawk appears fierce. The long neck and delicate plumes of the egret give it a stately appearance, while the facial discs of an owl create an apathetic gaze. All these and other impressions arouse emotions within us, and it is these arousals that will often sell the piece of art to a customer or capture a ribbon at competition.

With so many techniques and styles prominent in the carving field, no attempt will be made to tell you "how," but rather try to give you the structural basics about birds. There are numerous books available about birds and bird carving, but there is no substitute for practice. Nor is there any better way to learn about birds than to observe them in their natural habitat.

Armed with a pair of binoculars, notebook, pencil, and perhaps a camera, a walk in the field (or just the backyard) can prove to be an invaluable learning experience about birds. Zoos, aviaries, and rehabilitation centers are other good sources of learning by watching. Many museums have collections of study skins that often may be available for use simply by making a phone call to arrange access to them.

A taxidermy mount of the species you are going to carve can be quite valuable, but bear in mind that a taxidermist is also an artist and sometimes depicts the species as he or she may interpret it. Castings of bills are available from most supply houses and provide an excellent source of reference. These bills are cast from bird specimens and usually show extreme details that often are not apparent in photographs.

More than nine thousand different species of birds are presently recorded with more being discovered each day. Ornithologists and naturalists are having a heyday in the rain forests of South America and the outback of Australia. It appears that the wildfowl carver and artist will have a never-ending reference source of our fine feathered friends.

Self Test

1. The "map" of the surface areas of a bird is called _____.

2. The "orbital region" includes the _____ , _____ , and _____.

3. The _____ are commonly called the ear coverts.

4. The large orbital area of many owls is called the _____.

5. The two main parts of the bill are the _____ and the _____.

6. A feather follicle is a bacterial infection. (True or False)

7. Areas on a bird where feathers do not grow are called _____ .

8. The colored part of the eye is the _____.

9. A bird looks in different directions by _____.

10. Most predators have eyes set for _____ vision.

11. The "third eyelid" on a bird is the _____.

12. How many feather tracts are found on the head of a bird and what are their names?

    _____.

13. When the malar region is a distinctively different color, it is called the

    _____ .

14. Ear tufts are the feathers that cover the ears. (True or False)

15. The iridescent bib of a hummingbird is called the _____ .

16. The eye of a bird is ball-shaped, or globular, the same as in humans. (True or False)

17. The fleshy pouch on the lower mandible of a pelican is correctly called a

    _____ .

18. The pendant of skin growing from the forehead and drooping over the bill of the wild turkey is called a _____ .

19. The area that a bird sees with both eyes is known as _____ .

20. What are the nasal canthus and the temporal canthus?

Answers on page 85

Glossary

Accommodation. The action of focusing the eye to accommodate near or distant vision.

Acute. A bill characteristic where the bill comes to a sharp point, as in the yellow warbler.

Aigrettes. A group of plumes; this was the primary feature used in naming egrets.

Air sacs. Bladderlike sacs in the respiratory system of a bird, which often are inflated during nuptial displays.

Angle-of-the-jaw. The angle formed by the joint of the lower mandible and the quadrate bone.

Angulated commissure. A bill characteristic where the commissure has a definite downward angle at the rictus.

Apteria. The featherless or bald areas on the skin of a bird.

Aqueous humor. The fluid-filled space between the cornea and the iris of the eye.

Articulated. A movable joint of the skeleton.

Atlas. The first vertebra of the neck which forms a joint with the occipital condoyle.

Auricular region. Topographically, the area of the ears.

Auriculars. The feathers that cover the ear opening.

Axis. The second vertebra of the neck upon which the atlas rotates.

Bent. A bill shape that has a prominent angle or bend, as seen in flamingos.

Bib. Topographically, the area just below the chin of a bird—often a different color as in the ruby-throated hummingbird; see also GORGET.

Binocular vision. The area that a bird sees with both eyes—as opposed to monocular vision.

Biochromes. A type of color pigment that relates to true color as opposed to color produced by light diffraction.

Brevis. Latin word meaning brief or short; used extensively in naming muscles.

Bristles. A hairlike type of feather.

Capital tract. The feather tract on the top of the head.

Carotenoids. A type of color pigment; see also MELANINS.

Caruncles. Fleshy outgrowths of the skin, usually brightly colored, wrinkled, or wartlike in appearance; see also WATTLES and COMB.

Casque. A horny outgrowth of the skull in the region of the forehead, as in cassowaries.

Cere. See OPERCULUM.

Cervical column. All the bones, collectively, that make up the neck of a bird.

Cervical vertebrae. The individual bones of the neck.

Cheek. See MALAR REGION.

Chemical coloration. A method by which feathers and other parts get their color from chemical pigments called biochromes.

Chin. Topographically, the feathered area in the forked portion, on the underside of the lower mandible.

Chisel-like. A bill shape where the tip of the bill is beveled, as in the hairy woodpecker.

Choroid. The middle of three layers that form the rear wall of the eye.

Ciliary body. The structural part of the eye that supports and focuses the lens.

Circular. A nostril shape that is more or less round.

Comb. A fleshy outgrowth on the crown of some species so named because of its serrated edge, as in the domestic chicken.

Commissure. The line formed where the upper and lower mandibles meet; see also GAPE.

Compressed. A bill shape where the bill is higher than it is wide, as in puffins.

Cones. Found in the retina, these are the visual image receptors that are highly sensitive to daylight; see also RODS.

Conical. A bill shape that is apparently cone shaped or having an even taper, as that of the redpoll.

Cornea. The transparent front wall of the eye.

Cranial kinesis. A movement between parts of the cranium that is dependant upon an external force being applied to the parts; e.g., movement of the upper mandible with respect to the skull.

Cranium. Collectively, all the bones that unite to form the brain cavity.

Crest. A group of elongated, erect feathers growing on the crown as in the cardinal.

Crossed. A bill shape where the tips of the upper and lower mandible overlap like a pair of shears.

Crown. Topographically, the top of the head; see also CREST.

Culmen. The centerline ridge of the upper mandible.

Decurved. A bill shape where the bill has an obvious downward curve, as in the curlew.

Depressed. A bill shape where the bill is obviously wider than it is high, as in ducks.

Dermis. The secondary or underlayer of the skin.

Dewlap. A wattle that grows from the chin or gular region; see also LAPPET.

Diopter. A unit of measurement of the refractive power of lenses equal to the reciprocal of the focal length in meters.

Dorsal tract. The feather tract on the top side of a bird; see also SPINAL TRACT.

Ear coverts. See AURICULARS.

Ear tufts. A group of erect feathers growing above the eyes that resemble ears on a bird.

Epidermis. The surface layer of the skin.

Extensor. A muscle that extends or straightens the angle of a joint.

Eye stripe. A line of feathers above the eye that is a distinctively different color than the surrounding feathers.

Eye-ring. The feathered area surrounding the eyelids, sometimes a different color than the other feathers of the head.

Eyelashes. Bristle-type feathers that grow on the eyelid, as seen in the ostrich.

Eyelids. Folds of skin directly above and below the eye; see also NICTITATING MEMBRANE.

Facia. A sheet of connective tissue that envelopes a muscle or other part of the body. Facia also joins the skin to the body.

Facial disc. In owls, a circular group of feathers with a disclike shape, which surrounds the eye.

Feather follicle. A cavity or depression in the skin from which a feather grows.

Feather groups. Feathers that grow in a particular segment of a feather tract, such as the auriculars, ear tufts, crests, etc.

Feather tract. An area of a bird from which particular groups of feathers grow, such as the capital tract, crural tract, humeral tract, and so on.

Flexor. A muscle that bends or reduces the angle of a joint.

Forehead. Topographically, the area of the head from the base of the upper bill to an imaginary line connecting the front corners of the eyes.

Fovea. An area or spot on the retina that contains high concentrations of rods or cones to receive extremely sharp visual images. Many birds have more than one fovea in each eye.

Frontals. The bones that unite to make up the forehead of a bird's skull.

Frontal shield. A horny covering of the forehead, as seen in coots.

Gape. Usually referring to the open mouth, this is the line created along the edges of the open bill; see also COMMISSURE.

Gibbous. A bill shape that has an apparent hump on the upper mandible, as in the scoter.

Gorget. In hummingbirds, the iridescent feathers of the throat area, often extending far to the sides of the neck.

Gular region. Anatomically, the area of the throat, just below the chin and extending to the breast.

Gular sac. A fleshy pouch of the gular region, as seen in pelicans.

Gular tract. A division of the ventral tract, located on the underside of the neck and considered by some authorities to be a separate tract.

Herbst corpuscles. Found primarily in the bills and feet of birds, these corpuscles are what is believed to make these parts sensitive to touch.

Hindhead. See OCCIPUT.

Homologous. Structurally similar to; as the leg of a bird is homologous to the leg of man.

Hooked. A bill shape where the upper mandible is longer than the lower and has a definite curve, or hook, at the tip, as seen in hawks.

Hyoid apparatus. Collectively, all the bones of the tongue.

Imperforate. When the nostrils are separated internally by a nasal septum they are said to be imperforate.

Integument. A term referring to the outer covering of a bird or animal and includes the skin, hair, feathers, scales, claws, and bill covering.

Interorbital septum. A vertical, platelike bone that separates the two orbits or eye cavities.

Iridescence. A color characteristic, normally in feathers, caused by light diffraction.

Iris. The colored part of the eye.

Joint. The point where two bones meet. There are two types of joints: the suture and the articulated.

Jugulum. Topographically, the underside of the neck, extending from the malar region to the breast; the throat.

Keratin. Found in the integument of a bird, this compound is used for the formation of feathers and the horny growth of the ramphotheca.

Lacrimals. A pair of bones, one on each side of the face, that make the foundation for the lores.

Lamellate. A bill that has toothlike ridges just inside the cutting edges, as seen in ducks and flamingos.

Lappet. A wattle growing from the corner of the mouth of a bird; see also DEWLAP and RICTAL WATTLE.

Leader. A pendant-type caruncle growing from the forehead of the wild turkey; see also SNOOD.

Lens. The part of the eye that is changed in shape to focus visual images upon the retina.

Light interference. A method by which certain colors are produced by light diffraction; see also IRIDESCENCE.

Linear. A nostril shape that somewhat resembles a slit, as in gulls.

Long. A bill shape where the bill is considerably longer than the head, as in curlews.

Longus. Latin terminology meaning long, as opposed to brevis. Used extensively in the naming of muscles.

Lore. Topographically, the area between the upper mandible and the eye.

Lower mandible. The bottom half of the bill.

Magnus. Latin terminology meaning large; used extensively in naming muscles.

Malar patch. When the malar region is a distinctively different color than the surrounding feathers it is called a malar patch; also referred to as the "mustache."

Malar region. Topographically, the area below the lores at the base of the lower mandible and extending to a point just behind and below the ears. Sometimes called the "cheek."

Malars. Feathers growing in the malar region.

Maxilla. The two primary bones of the upper mandible; commonly used term referring to the upper part of the bill or upper mandible.

Melanins. A type of color pigment; see also CAROTENOIDS.

Minimus. Latin terminology meaning small, or minimal; used extensively in naming muscles.

Monocular vision. The area that is seen with only one eye, as opposed to binocular vision.

Mustache. See MALAR PATCH.

Myopic. Being nearsighted or able to see clearly only at very close proximity to an object.

Nail. A hard projection on the tip of the upper mandible, as seen on ducks.

Nail tooth. A hard toothlike projection found on the ventral side, at the tip, of the upper mandible of newly hatched chicks. The nail tooth is used to help break the eggshell for hatching and usually disappears in a few days.

Nape. Topographically, the area of the dorsal side of the neck, extending from the head to the body.

Nares. On the surface of the bill, the openings to the nostrils.

Nasal canthus. The front corner of the eye, closest to the nostrils, where the upper and lower eyelids meet.

Nasal septum. The platelike bone separating the two nasal passages. Not all species have a nasal septum.

Nasals. The bones that form the nasal passages.

Nictitating membrane. A semi-transparent membrane under the eyelids, at the nasal canthus, used for blinking, cleaning, and moistening the eye; see also THIRD EYELID.

Nostrils. Openings in the upper mandible through which air passes for the purpose of breathing; see also NARES.

Notched. A bill characteristic where the upper mandible has a notch, or tooth, near the tip, as seen in falcons.

Occipital. The bone that forms the rear part of the cranium.

Occipital condoyle. A ball-like projection on the ventral side of the occipital bone that forms an articulated joint with the atlas.

Occiput. Topographically, the sloping hind part of the head.

Operculate. Having an operculum or cere.

Operculum. A swollen, fleshy mass at the base of the upper mandible that totally or partially covers the nostrils, as in the pigeon.

Optic nerve. Connected to the eye, this nerve transmits the visual image to the brain.

Orbit. See ORBITAL CAVITY.

Orbital. Referring to the area of the eye.

Orbital cavity. In the skull, the socket for the eye.

Orbital region. Topographically, the area surrounding and including the eye, eyelids, and eye-ring.

Oval. A nostril shape that is somewhat teardrop shaped.

Parietals. A pair of bones of the cranium that cover the front of the brain cavity and form the base of the forehead.

Pecten. A structure that projects, internally, from the retina and supplies nutrients to the eye of a bird.

Perforate. When the nasal passages are not separated by a septum, or bone partition, they are said to be perforate.

Pigments. Found in the skin and feathers, these are what produce true color.

Plume. A type of long, fluffy feather, as seen on the head and neck of egrets.

Pneumatized. Containing numerous air cavities. The skull of a bird is highly pneumatized, as are the bones.

Pterylae. Areas on the skin where feathers grow, as opposed to apteria.

Pupil. The aperture or opening of the iris through which light passes to cast a visual image on the retina.

Quadrate. A bone that links the skull and the lower mandible; see also ANGLE-OF-THE-JAW.

Quadratojugal. A pair of long, thin bones on either side of the upper mandible that join at the angle-of-the-jaw; see also QUADRATE and ZYGOMATIC BAR.

Ramphotheca. The horny covering of the bone structure of the upper and lower mandible.

Ramus. Term for the entire bill.

Recurved. A bill shape where the bill obviously curves upward at the tip, as in the American avocet.

Retina. The inner layer of a three-layer wall at the back of the eye. The retina receives the visual image of what the eye sees.

Rhodopsin. A reddish pigment (visual purple) in the retina that is largely responsible for nocturnal vision.

Rictal wattle. Pendantlike flaps of skin growing from the rictals, or corner of the mouth, as in the wild turkey; see also LAPPET.

Rods. Visual reception cells of the retina. Rods are especially sensitive in dim light; see also CONES.

Sclera. The outermost of the three layers that make up the rear wall of the eye.

Scleral ossicles. The individual bones that make up the sclerotic ring.

Sclerotic ring. A ring of platelike bones encircling the eye.

Septum. A platelike dividing wall between two chambers, such as the orbital septum, which separates the two eye sockets.

Short. A bill shape where the bill length is obviously shorter than the head, as in chickadees.

Sides. In topography, the area on each side of the neck between the nape and the jugulum.

Sieve-billed. See LAMELLATE.

Skull. Collectively, all the bones of the head.

Snood. A pendant-type caruncle growing from the forehead of the wild turkey; see also LEADER.

Spatulate. A bill shape where the tip is extremely wide and flattened, as in spoonbills.

Sphenoid. The bone that makes up the floor of the cranium or brain cavity.

Spinal tract. A division of the dorsal tract that covers the back, or spine, of a bird.

Spoon-shaped. See SPATULATE.

Squamosals. A pair of bones, one on each side of the head, that help form the cranium.

Stout. A bill shape that is obviously high and wide, as in a grouse.

Straight. A bill characteristic where the bill is in line with the head, as in the bittern.

Structural coloration. Color produced by the structure of a feather, as opposed to chemical coloration.

Superciliary line. An imaginary topographical line on the head marking the lateral extent of the forehead, crown, and occiput.

Suture. A type of joint where the bones do not articulate, or move, with respect to each other.

Swollen. A bill shape where the bill is somewhat bulged at the sides, as in a tanager.

Temporal canthus. The rear corner of the eye where the upper and lower eyelids meet; closest to the temporal region.

Temporal region. Topographically, the area just behind the eye and above the ear opening; normally considered as part of the auricular region.

Terete. A bill shape that is round in cross-section, as in the hummingbird.

Third eyelid. See NICTITATING MEMBRANE.

Throat wattle. See DEWLAP.

Tract. See FEATHER TRACT.

Upper mandible. The top or upper half of the bill.

Ventral tract. The primary feather tract on the underside of a bird.

Vertebral column. Collectively, all the bones comprising the spine, or backbone, of a bird or animal.

Visual acuity. The ability to see things clearly.

Visual field. The area that the eye can see; see also MONOCULAR and BINOCULAR VISION.

Wattles. Pendant-type caruncles, usually brightly colored, growing from the skin on the head of a bird; see also DEWLAP and LAPPET.

Zygomatic bar. A group of long, thin bones of the upper mandible that join with the quadrate bone at the angle-of-the-jaw; see also QUADRATOJUGAL.

Bibliography

Although a great number of sources were used as reference material for this book, the primary sources were as follows:

Brooke, M., and T. Birkhead, eds. *Cambridge Encyclopedia of Ornithology*. New York: Cambridge Press, 1991.

Burne, David. *Bird*. Eyewitness Books. London: Dorling Kindersly Ltd., 1988.

Farner, D. S., J. R. King Jr., and K. C. Parkes, eds. *Avian Biology*. 2 vols. New York: Academic Press, 1971.

Pasquier, Roger R. *Watching Birds: An Introduction to Ornithology*. Boston: Houghton Mifflin Co., 1977.

Peterson, Roger Tory. *The Birds*. Life Nature Library. New York: Time Inc., 1963.

Pettingill, O. S., Jr., *Ornithology in Laboratory and Field*. Orlando, Fla.: Academic Press, 1985.

Terres, J. K. *Encyclopedia of North American Birds*. New York: Wings Books, 1991.

VanTyne, J., and A. J. Berger. *Fundamentals of Ornithology*. New York: Dover Publications, 1971.

TEST ANSWERS

1. topography

2. eye, eyelids, and eye-ring

3. auriculars

4. facial disc

5. upper mandible, lower mandible

6. False. A feather follicle is the socket from which a feather grows.

7. apteria

8. iris

9. turning the head and neck

10. forward

11. nictitating membrane

12. Two. The capital tract and the ventral tract.

13. malar patch or mustache

14 False. Ear tufts are erect tufts of feathers on the head that resemble ears. Auriculars are the feathers that cover the ears of a bird.

15. gorget

16. False. The eye of a bird is somewhat pear-shaped.

17. gular sac

18. snood or leader

19. binocular vision

20. The front and rear corners of the eye, where the upper and lower eyelids meet.

ABOUT THE AUTHOR

Jack Kochan is a veteran bird carver whose interest in the hobby was sparked ten years ago by a visit to a decoy factory. Since then his carvings have earned numerous awards, including first-place honors at the Ward World Championships in 1990. He credits his success to his knowledge of avian anatomy, which he says helps him create detailed, lifelike carvings. As an artist and illustrator, Kochan has produced work for a variety of publications. An avid outdoorsman, he lives in Leesport, Pennsylvania.